Contents

Party-Time Dips

**A VARIETY OF HOT AND COLD DIPS
TO JUMP-START YOUR NEXT CELEBRATION**

VELVEETA Ultimate Queso Dip

Prep: 5 min. ● Total: 10 min.

1 lb. (16 oz.) **VELVEETA** Pasteurized Prepared Cheese Product,
   cut into ½-inch cubes

1 can (10 oz.) RO*TEL® Diced Tomatoes & Green Chilies,
   undrained

MIX VELVEETA and tomatoes in microwaveable bowl.

MICROWAVE on HIGH 5 min. or until **VELVEETA** is completely
melted, stirring after 3 min.

SERVE with tortilla chips or assorted cut-up vegetables.

Makes 3 cups or 24 servings,
2 Tbsp. each.

SIZE-WISE:

When eating appetizers at social occasions, preview your choices and
decide which you'd like to try instead of taking some of each.

CREATIVE LEFTOVERS:

Cover and refrigerate any leftover dip. Reheat and serve over hot baked
potatoes or cooked pasta.

SUBSTITUTE:

Prepare as directed, using VELVEETA Mild Mexican Pasteurized Prepared
Cheese Product with Jalapeño Peppers.

*Ro*Tel® is a product of ConAgra Foods, Inc.*

VELVEETA Chili Dip

Prep: 5 min. • Total: 10 min.

- 1 lb. (16 oz.) **VELVEETA** Pasteurized Prepared Cheese Product, cut into ½-inch cubes
- 1 can (15 oz.) chili with or without beans

MIX VELVEETA and chili in microwaveable bowl. Microwave on HIGH 5 min. or until **VELVEETA** is completely melted and mixture is well blended, stirring after 3 min.

SERVE hot with tortilla chips, **RITZ** Toasted Chips or assorted cut-up vegetables.

Makes 3 cups or 24 servings, 2 Tbsp. each.

HEALTHY LIVING:

Save 20 calories and 2 grams of fat per serving by preparing with VELVEETA Made With 2% Milk Reduced Fat Pasteurized Prepared Cheese Product.

HOW TO HALVE:

Mix ½ lb. (8 oz.) VELVEETA Pasteurized Prepared Cheese Product, cut up, and ¾ cup canned chili in 1-qt. microwaveable bowl. Microwave on HIGH 3 to 4 min. or until VELVEETA is melted, stirring after 2 min. Serve as directed. Makes 1¼ cups or 10 servings, 2 Tbsp. each.

TO SERVE A CROWD:

Mix 1½ lb. (24 oz.) VELVEETA Pasteurized Prepared Cheese Product, cut up, and 2 cups canned chili in 2½-qt microwaveable bowl on HIGH 4 min.; stir. Microwave 4 to 6 min. or until VELVEETA is melted, stirring every 2 min.; stir. Serve as directed. Makes 5 cups or 40 servings, 2 Tbsp. each.

VELVEETA Ranch Dip

Prep: 5 min. • Total: 11 min.

- 1 lb. (16 oz.) **VELVEETA** Pasteurized Prepared Cheese Product, cut into ½-inch cubes
- 1 container (8 oz.) **BREAKSTONE'S** or **KNUDSEN** Sour Cream
- 1 cup **KRAFT** Ranch Dressing

MIX all ingredients in microwaveable bowl.

MICROWAVE on HIGH 6 min. or until **VELVEETA** is completely melted and mixture is well blended, stirring every 2 min.

SERVE with assorted cut-up vegetables or your favorite **NABISCO** Crackers.

Makes 3¼ cups or 26 servings, 2 Tbsp. each.

VELVEETA ZESTY RANCH DIP:

Add 1 can (10 oz.) undrained RO*TEL® Diced Tomatoes and Green Chilies to dip ingredients before microwaving. Increase the microwave time to 8 min., stirring every 2 min. Serve as directed.

VELVEETA PEPPER JACK RANCH DIP:

Prepare as directed, using VELVEETA Pepper Jack Pasteurized Prepared Cheese Product.

HOW TO SERVE IT COLD:

This versatile dip can also be served cold. Just prepare as directed; cool completely. Cover and refrigerate several hours or until chilled. Serve as directed.

*Ro*Tel® is a product of ConAgra Foods, Inc.*

VELVEETA Cheesy Bean Dip

Prep: 5 min. ● Total: 11 min.

- 1 lb. (16 oz.) **VELVEETA** Mild Mexican Pasteurized Prepared Cheese Product with Jalapeño Peppers, cut into ½-inch cubes
- 1 can (16 oz.) **TACO BELL® HOME ORIGINALS®** Refried Beans
- ½ cup **TACO BELL® HOME ORIGINALS®** Thick 'N Chunky Salsa

MIX all ingredients in microwaveable bowl.

MICROWAVE on HIGH 5 to 6 min. or until **VELVEETA** is completely melted and mixture is well blended, stirring after 3 min.

SERVE hot with tortilla chips or assorted cut-up vegetables.

Makes 3¼ cups or 26 servings, 2 Tbsp. each.

USE YOUR STOVE:

Mix all ingredients in medium saucepan. Cook on medium-low heat until VELVEETA is completely melted and mixture is well blended, stirring frequently. Serve as directed.

BEAN DIP OLÉ:

Prepare as directed, omitting the salsa, using VELVEETA Pasteurized Prepared Cheese Product and adding 1 undrained 4-oz. can chopped green chilies.

JAZZ IT UP:

To serve in a bread bowl, cut a lengthwise slice from the top of 1 (1-lb.) round bread loaf. Remove center of loaf, leaving 1-inch-thick shell. Cut loaf top and remove bread into bite-sized pieces to serve with dip. Fill bread bowl with hot dip just before serving.

TACO BELL® and HOME ORIGINALS® are trademarks owned and licensed by Taco Bell Corp.

Hot Broccoli Dip

Prep: 30 min. • Total: 30 min.

- 1 loaf (1½ lb.) round sourdough bread
- ½ cup chopped celery
- ½ cup chopped red bell peppers
- ¼ cup chopped onions
- 2 Tbsp. butter or margarine
- 1 lb. (16 oz.) **VELVEETA** Pasteurized Prepared Cheese Product, cut into ½-inch cubes
- 1 pkg. (10 oz.) frozen chopped broccoli, thawed, drained
- ¼ tsp. dried rosemary leaves, crushed

    Few drops hot pepper sauce

PREHEAT oven to 350°F. Cut slice from top of bread loaf; remove center, leaving 1-inch-thick shell. Cut removed bread into bite-sized pieces. Cover shell with top of bread; place on baking sheet with bread pieces. Bake 15 min. Cool slightly.

MEANWHILE, cook and stir celery, red bell peppers and onions in butter in medium saucepan on medium heat until tender. Reduce heat to low. Add **VELVEETA**; cook until melted, stirring frequently. Add broccoli, rosemary and hot pepper sauce; mix well. Cook until heated through, stirring constantly.

SPOON into bread loaf. Serve hot with toasted bread pieces, **NABISCO** Crackers and/or assorted cut-up vegetables.

Makes 2½ cups or 20 servings, 2 Tbsp. each.

USE YOUR MICROWAVE:

Mix celery, red bell peppers, onions and butter in 2-qt. microwaveable bowl. Microwave on HIGH 1 min. Add VELVEETA, broccoli, rosemary and hot pepper sauce; mix well. Microwave 5 to 6 min. or until VELVEETA is melted, stirring after 3 min.

VARIATION:

Omit bread loaf. Spoon dip into serving bowl. Serve with crackers and assorted cut-up vegetables as directed.

SUBSTITUTE:

Prepare as directed, using VELVEETA Made With 2% Milk Reduced Fat Pasteurized Prepared Cheese Product.

VELVEETA Salsa Dip

Prep: 5 min. ● Total: 10 min.

1 lb. (16 oz.) **VELVEETA** Pasteurized Prepared Cheese Product,
   cut into ½-inch cubes

1 cup **TACO BELL® HOME ORIGINALS®** Thick 'N Chunky Salsa

COMBINE ingredients in microwaveable bowl. Microwave on HIGH
5 min. or until **VELVEETA** is completely melted and mixture is well
blended, stirring after 3 min.

SERVE hot with tortilla chips, assorted cut-up fresh vegetables or
RITZ Toasted Chips Original.

Makes 2½ cups or 20 servings, 2 Tbsp. each.

HEALTHY LIVING:

Save 20 calories and 2.5 g of fat per serving by preparing with VELVEETA
Made With 2% Milk Reduced Fat Pasteurized Prepared Cheese Product.

HOW TO CUT UP VELVEETA:

Cut VELVEETA (the whole loaf) into ½-inch-thick slices. Then, cut each slice
crosswise in both directions to make cubes.

VELVEETA MEXICAN SALSA DIP:

Prepare as directed, using VELVEETA Mild Mexican Pasteurized Prepared
Cheese Product with Jalapeño Peppers.

*TACO BELL® and HOME ORIGINALS® are trademarks owned and licensed by
Taco Bell Corp.*

VELVEETA Spicy Sausage Dip

Prep: 5 min. ● Total: 10 min.

- 1 lb. (16 oz.) **VELVEETA** Pasteurized Prepared Cheese Product, cut into ½-inch cubes
- ½ lb. pork sausage, cooked, drained
- 1 can (10 oz.) RO*TEL® Diced Tomatoes & Green Chilies, undrained

MICROWAVE all ingredients in large microwaveable bowl on HIGH 5 min. or until **VELVEETA** is completely melted, stirring after 3 min.

SERVE hot with tortilla chips or **WHEAT THINS** Snack Crackers.

Makes 1 qt. or 32 servings,
2 Tbsp. each.

STORAGE KNOW-HOW:

Store leftover dip in airtight container in refrigerator up to 3 days. Reheat dip in microwave before serving.

*Ro*Tel® is a product of ConAgra Foods, Inc.*

Cheesy Spinach and Bacon Dip

Prep: 10 min. ● Total: 10 min.

1 pkg. (10 oz.) frozen chopped spinach, thawed, drained

1 lb. (16 oz.) **VELVEETA** Pasteurized Prepared Cheese Product, cut into ½-inch cubes

4 oz. (½ of 8-oz. pkg.) **PHILADELPHIA** Cream Cheese, cut up

1 can (10 oz.) RO*TEL® Diced Tomatoes & Green Chilies, undrained

8 slices **OSCAR MAYER** Bacon, crisply cooked, drained and crumbled

COMBINE ingredients in microwaveable bowl.

MICROWAVE on HIGH 5 min. or until **VELVEETA** is completely melted and mixture is well blended, stirring after 3 min.

Makes 4 cups or 32 servings, 2 Tbsp. each.

VARIATION:

Prepare as directed, using VELVEETA Made With 2% Milk Reduced Fat Pasteurized Prepared Cheese Product and PHILADELPHIA Neufchâtel Cheese, ⅓ Less Fat than Cream Cheese.

HOW TO CUT UP VELVEETA:

Cut VELVEETA (the whole loaf) into ½-inch-thick slices. Then, cut each slice crosswise in both directions to make cubes.

CREATIVE LEFTOVERS:

Cover and refrigerate any leftover dip. Then, reheat and toss with your favorite hot, cooked pasta.

*Ro*Tel® is a product of ConAgra Foods, Inc.*

Cheesy Hawaiian Dip

Prep: 20 min. ● Total: 20 min.

1 round loaf Hawaiian bread (1 lb.)

1 lb. (16 oz.) **VELVEETA** Pasteurized Prepared Cheese Product, cut into ½-inch cubes

1 can (10 oz.) RO*TEL® Diced Tomatoes & Green Chilies, undrained

⅓ cup chopped red onions

1 pkg. (8 oz.) **OSCAR MAYER** Smoked Ham, chopped

1 can (8 oz.) crushed pineapple, drained

PREHEAT oven to 350°F. Cut slice from top of bread loaf; remove center of loaf, leaving 1-inch-thick shell. Place on baking sheet. Cut removed bread into bite-size pieces. Place in single layer around bread shell on baking sheet. Bake 8 to 10 min. or until lightly toasted, stirring cubes after 5 min. Cool slightly.

MEANWHILE mix **VELVEETA**, tomatoes and onions in large microwaveable bowl. Microwave on HIGH 5 min. or until **VELVEETA** is completely melted, stirring after 3 min. Stir in ham and pineapple. Pour into bread shell.

SERVE with reserved bread pieces and assorted fresh vegetable dippers.

Makes 4½ cups or 36 servings, 2 Tbsp. each.

SUBSTITUTE:

Prepare as directed, using VELVEETA Made With 2% Milk Reduced Fat Pasteurized Prepared Cheese Product.

CREATIVE LEFTOVERS:

Cover and refrigerate any leftover dip. Reheat and use as a cheesy sauce for hot baked potatoes or steamed broccoli florets.

*Ro*Tel® is a product of ConAgra Foods, Inc.*

VELVEETA Spicy Buffalo Dip

Prep: 5 min. • Total: 10 min.

1 lb. (16 oz.) **VELVEETA** Pasteurized Prepared Cheese Product, cut into ½-inch cubes

1 cup **BREAKSTONE'S** or **KNUDSEN** Sour Cream

¼ cup cayenne pepper sauce for Buffalo wings

¼ cup **KRAFT** Natural Blue Cheese Crumbles

2 green onions, sliced

COMBINE VELVEETA, sour cream and pepper sauce in large microwaveable bowl. Microwave on HIGH 5 min. or until **VELVEETA** is completely melted, stirring after 3 min.

STIR in remaining ingredients.

SERVE hot with celery and carrot sticks.

Makes 2¾ cups or 22 servings, 2 Tbsp. each.

VARIATION:

Prepare as directed, using VELVEETA Made With 2% Milk Reduced Fat Pasteurized Prepared Cheese Product and BREAKSTONE'S Reduced Fat or KNUDSEN Light Sour Cream.

SERVE IT COLD:

This dip is also great served cold. Prepare as directed; cool. Cover and refrigerate several hours or until chilled. Serve as directed.

KEEPING IT SAFE:

Hot dips should be discarded after setting at room temperature for 2 hours or longer.

Awesome Appetizers & Snacks

EASY-TO-MAKE POTATO SKINS, NACHOS, QUESADILLAS AND MORE

Cheesy Franks

Prep: 5 min. • Total: 15 min.

6 **OSCAR MAYER** Wieners

6 oz. **VELVEETA** Pasteurized Prepared Cheese Product, cut into
   ½-inch cubes

2 Tbsp. milk

2 Tbsp. chopped green onions

6 hot dog buns, split

HEAT wieners as directed on package or grill until heated through
(160°F).

PLACE VELVEETA in saucepan. Add milk; cook on low heat until
VELVEETA is completely melted and mixture is well blended,
stirring frequently. Stir in onions.

FILL buns with wieners; top with **VELVEETA** mixture.

Makes 6 servings, 1 frank each.

SERVING SUGGESTION:

Serve these fun franks with assorted cut-up vegetables and a piece of
fruit.

HOW TO SLICE VELVEETA EASILY:

Spray knife blade with a light mist of nonstick cooking spray first. No
more sticking!

Crispy Tostadas

Prep: 10 min. • Total: 17 min.

8 tostada shells (5 inch)

1 can (16 oz.) **TACO BELL® HOME ORIGINALS®** Refried Beans

1 cup finely chopped red and green bell peppers

½ lb. (8 oz.) **VELVEETA** Pepper Jack Pasteurized Prepared
   Cheese Product, sliced

1 cup shredded lettuce

½ cup **TACO BELL® HOME ORIGINALS®** Thick 'N Chunky Salsa

PREHEAT oven to 350°F. Spread tostada shells with beans; top
evenly with bell peppers and **VELVEETA**.

BAKE 5 to 7 min. or until **VELVEETA** is melted.

TOP with lettuce and salsa.

Makes 8 servings, 1 tostada each.

VARIATION-CRISPY BEEF TOSTADAS:

Omit refried beans. Brown 1 lb. lean ground beef in medium skillet; drain.
Return to skillet. Add 1 pkg. (1¼ oz.) TACO BELL® HOME ORIGINALS® Taco
Seasoning Mix; prepare as directed on package. Spoon meat mixture
evenly onto tostada shells. Top with peppers and VELVEETA. Continue as
directed.

SERVING SUGGESTION:

Serve with a tossed green salad drizzled with KRAFT Light Ranch Reduced
Fat Dressing.

*TACO BELL® and HOME ORIGINALS® are trademarks owned and licensed by
Taco Bell Corp.*

VELVEETA Double-Decker Nachos

Prep: 15 min. ● Total: 15 min.

- 6 oz. tortilla chips (about 7 cups)
- 1 can (15 oz.) chili with beans
- ½ lb. (8 oz.) **VELVEETA** Pasteurized Prepared Cheese Product, cut into ½-inch cubes
- 1 medium tomato, finely chopped
- ¼ cup sliced green onions
- ⅓ cup **BREAKSTONE'S** or **KNUDSEN** Sour Cream

ARRANGE half of the chips on large microwaveable platter; top with layers of half *each* of the chili and **VELVEETA**. Repeat layers.

MICROWAVE on HIGH 3 to 5 min. or until **VELVEETA** is melted.

TOP with remaining ingredients.

Makes 6 servings.

SIZE-WISE:

Enjoy your favorite foods while keeping portion size in mind.

SUBSTITUTE:

Prepare as directed, using VELVEETA Mild Mexican Pasteurized Prepared Cheese Product with Jalapeño Peppers.

Chimichangas

Prep: 15 min. ● Total: 55 min. (incl. refrigerating)

1 lb. ground beef

½ cup finely chopped onions

2 cloves garlic, minced

1 tsp. dried oregano leaves

1 tsp. crushed red pepper

6 oz. **VELVEETA** Pasteurized Prepared Cheese Product, cut into 8 slices

8 **TACO BELL® HOME ORIGINALS®** Flour Tortillas

2 cups oil

¼ cup **BREAKSTONE'S** or **KNUDSEN** Sour Cream

¼ cup finely chopped fresh cilantro

BROWN meat in large skillet on medium-high heat; drain. Add onions, garlic, oregano and crushed red pepper; mix well. Cook until onions are tender, stirring occasionally; drain.

PLACE ¼ cup of the meat mixture and 1 **VELVEETA** slice in the center of each tortilla. Fold in all sides of tortillas to completely enclose filling; secure with wooden toothpicks. Place in single layer on baking sheet; cover. Refrigerate 20 min.

HEAT oil in large saucepan on medium-high heat. Add tortilla pouches, 2 at a time; cook 5 min. or until golden brown. Drain. Remove toothpicks. Top each serving with 1 Tbsp. *each* of the sour cream and cilantro.

Makes 4 servings, 2 chimichangas each.

VARIATION:

Save 110 calories and 14 g total fat per serving by substituting 1 lb. potatoes, cooked and cubed, for the browned ground beef and by using VELVEETA Made With 2% Milk Reduced Fat Pasteurized Prepared Process Cheese Product and BREAKSTONE'S Reduced Fat or KNUDSEN Light Sour Cream. To prepare, cook and stir onions with seasonings in large skillet 3 min. or until crisp-tender. Add potatoes; cook 3 to 5 min. or until potatoes are heated through, stirring frequently. Spoon onto tortillas and continue as directed.

Speedy Spicy Quesadillas

Prep: 5 min. ● Total: 8 min.

½ lb. (8 oz.) Mild **VELVEETA** Mexican Pasteurized Prepared
  Cheese Product with Jalapeño Peppers, cut into 8 slices

8 flour tortillas (6 inch)

PLACE 1 **VELVEETA** slice on each tortilla. Fold tortillas in half. Place 2 tortillas on microwaveable plate.

MICROWAVE on HIGH 30 to 45 sec. or until **VELVEETA** is melted. Repeat with remaining tortillas.

CUT each quesadilla in half. Serve immediately.

Makes 8 servings, 2 quesadilla halves each.

SUBSTITUTE:

Prepare as directed, using VELVEETA Made With 2% Milk Reduced Fat Pasteurized Prepared Cheese Product.

FOOD FACTS:

Flour tortillas, often used as soft taco shells, come in many colors and sizes. Look for them in the dairy case or grocery aisle of the supermarket. You'll also find them seasoned with herbs, tomatoes, spinach or sesame seeds.

JAZZ IT UP:

Garnish with chopped fresh tomatoes and green onions.

Bacon Cheeseburger Roll-Up

Prep: 25 min. ● Total: 50 min.

1 lb. lean ground beef

4 slices **OSCAR MAYER** Bacon, chopped

½ cup chopped onions (about 1 small)

½ lb. (8 oz.) **VELVEETA** Pasteurized Prepared Cheese Product, cut into ½-inch cubes

1 can (13.8 oz.) refrigerated pizza crust

PREHEAT oven to 400°F. Cook ground beef, bacon and onions in large skillet on medium-high heat until ground beef is evenly browned, stirring occasionally. Drain; return meat mixture to skillet. Add **VELVEETA**; cook until completely melted, stirring frequently. Cool 10 min.

UNROLL pizza dough onto baking sheet sprayed with cooking spray. Press into 15×8-inch rectangle. Top evenly with meat mixture. Roll up dough, starting at 1 of the long sides. Rearrange, if necessary, so roll is seam-side down on baking sheet.

BAKE 20 to 25 min. or until golden brown. Cut diagonally into 6 slices to serve.

Makes 6 servings, 1 slice each.

SERVING SUGGESTION:

Balance this indulgent "cheeseburger" with a mixed green salad and fresh fruit.

JAZZ IT UP:

Serve with your favorite condiments, such as CLAUSSEN Dill Burger Slices, mustard, ketchup, sliced tomatoes and/or TACO BELL® HOME ORIGINALS® Thick 'N Chunky Salsa.

VARIATION:

Prepare as directed, using VELVEETA Made With 2% Milk Reduced Fat Pasteurized Prepared Cheese Product and substituting 1 can (7 oz.) chopped mushrooms, drained, for the bacon.

TACO BELL® and HOME ORIGINALS® are trademarks owned and licensed by Taco Bell Corp.

Chicken Enchiladas

Prep: 20 min. ● Total: 40 min.

- 2 cups chopped cooked chicken or turkey
- 1 green bell pepper, chopped
- 4 oz. (½ of 8-oz. pkg.) **PHILADELPHIA** Cream Cheese, cubed
- ½ cup **TACO BELL® HOME ORIGINALS®** Thick 'N Chunky Salsa, divided
- 8 **TACO BELL® HOME ORIGINALS®** Flour Tortillas
- ¼ lb. (4 oz.) **VELVEETA** Pasteurized Prepared Cheese Product, cut into ½-inch cubes
- 1 Tbsp. milk

PREHEAT oven to 350°F. Mix chicken, green bell pepper, cream cheese and ¼ cup of the salsa in saucepan; cook on low heat until cream cheese is melted, stirring occasionally.

SPOON ⅓ cup of the chicken mixture down center of each tortilla; roll up. Place, seam-sides down, in lightly greased 13×9-inch baking dish. Place **VELVEETA** in small saucepan. Add milk; cook on low heat until **VELVEETA** is completely melted, stirring frequently. Pour over enchiladas; cover with foil.

BAKE 20 min. or until heated through. Top with remaining ¼ cup salsa.

Makes 4 servings, 2 enchiladas each.

SUBSTITUTE:

Prepare as directed, using PHILADELPHIA Neufchâtel Cheese, ⅓ Less Fat than Cream Cheese and VELVEETA Made With 2% Milk Reduced Fat Pasteurized Prepared Cheese Product.

SHORTCUT:

Substitute 1 pkg. (6 oz.) OSCAR MAYER Oven Roasted Chicken Breast Cuts for the chopped cooked fresh chicken.

TACO BELL® and HOME ORIGINALS® are trademarks owned and licensed by Taco Bell Corp.

Ultimate VELVEETA Nachos

Prep: 10 min. ● Total: 10 min.

- 1 lb. extra-lean ground beef
- 7 cups (6 oz.) tortilla chips
- ½ lb. (8 oz.) **VELVEETA** Pasteurized Prepared Cheese Product, cut into ½-inch cubes
- 1 cup shredded lettuce
- ½ cup chopped tomatoes
- ¼ cup sliced black olives
- ⅓ cup **BREAKSTONE'S** or **KNUDSEN** Sour Cream

BROWN meat; drain.

ARRANGE chips on microwaveable platter; top evenly with **VELVEETA**. Microwave on HIGH 2 min. or until **VELVEETA** is melted.

TOP with meat and remaining ingredients.

Makes 6 servings.

HEALTHY LIVING:

By preparing this dish with extra-lean ground beef (95% fat) instead of ground beef (80% fat), you will save 5g fat and 40 calories per serving.

JAZZ IT UP:

Season the meat with taco seasoning before spooning over the chips. Just brown the meat as directed. Then, add 1 pkg. (1¼ oz.) TACO BELL® HOME ORIGINALS® Taco Seasoning Mix and prepare as directed on package.

TACO BELL® and HOME ORIGINALS® are trademarks owned and licensed by Taco Bell Corp.

Awesome Appetizers & Snacks

Crowd-Pleasing Entrées

HEARTY DISHES FOR ANY GET-TOGETHER

Macaroni and Cheese Dijon

Prep: 20 min. ● Total: 45 min.

1¼ cups milk

½ lb. (8 oz.) **VELVEETA** Pasteurized Prepared Cheese Product, cut into ½-inch cubes

2 Tbsp. **GREY POUPON** Dijon Mustard

6 slices **OSCAR MAYER** Bacon, cooked, drained and crumbled

⅓ cup green onion slices

⅛ tsp. ground red pepper (cayenne)

3½ cups tri-colored rotini pasta, cooked, drained

½ cup French fried onion rings

PREHEAT oven to 350°F. Mix milk, **VELVEETA** and mustard in medium saucepan; cook on low heat until **VELVEETA** is completely melted and mixture is well blended, stirring occasionally. Add bacon, green onions and pepper; mix lightly. Remove from heat. Add to pasta in large bowl; toss to coat.

SPOON into greased 2-qt. casserole dish; cover.

BAKE 15 to 20 min. or until heated through. Uncover; stir. Top with onion rings. Bake, uncovered, an additional 5 min. Let stand 10 min. before serving.

Makes 6 servings, 1 cup each.

MAKE IT EASY:

For easy crumbled bacon, use kitchen scissors to snip raw bacon into ½-inch pieces. Let pieces fall right into skillet, then cook until crisp and drain on paper towels.

VELVEETA Chicken Enchilada Casserole

Prep: 15 min. ● Total: 50 min.

¾ cup **TACO BELL® HOME ORIGINALS®** Thick 'N Chunky Salsa, divided

2 cups chopped cooked chicken

1 can (10¾ oz.) condensed cream of chicken soup

½ lb. (8 oz.) **VELVEETA** Mild Mexican Pasteurized Prepared Cheese Product with Jalapeño Peppers, cut into ½-inch cubes

6 corn tortillas (6 inch), cut in half

PREHEAT oven to 350°F. Reserve ¼ cup of the salsa for later use. Mix chicken, soup and **VELVEETA** until well blended. Spread 1 cup of the chicken mixture onto bottom of 8-inch square baking dish.

TOP with layers of 6 tortilla halves, ¼ cup of the remaining salsa and half of the remaining chicken mixture; repeat layers.

BAKE 30 to 35 min. or until heated through. Serve topped with the reserved ¼ cup salsa.

Makes 6 servings.

USE YOUR MICROWAVE:

Assemble as directed in 8-inch square microwaveable dish. Microwave on HIGH 10 to 14 min. or until heated through.

SERVING SUGGESTION:

Serve with bagged salad greens topped with your favorite KRAFT Dressing, such as Ranch.

TACO BELL® and HOME ORIGINALS® are trademarks owned and licensed by Taco Bell Corp.

VELVEETA Ultimate Macaroni & Cheese

Prep: 20 min. ● Total: 20 min.

2 cups (8 oz.) elbow macaroni, uncooked

¾ lb. (12 oz.) **VELVEETA** Pasteurized Prepared Cheese Product, cut into ½-inch cubes

⅓ cup milk

⅛ tsp. black pepper

COOK macaroni as directed on package; drain well. Return to pan.

ADD remaining ingredients; mix well. Cook on low heat until **VELVEETA** is completely melted and mixture is well blended, stirring frequently.

Makes 4 servings, 1 cup each.

HEALTHY LIVING:

Save 70 calories and 10 grams of fat per serving by preparing with VELVEETA Made With 2% Milk Reduced Fat Pasteurized Prepared Cheese Product.

VARIATION:

Prepare as directed. Pour into 2-qt. casserole dish. Bake at 350°F for 25 min.

DRESSED-UP MAC 'N CHEESE:

Substitute bow-tie pasta or your favorite shaped pasta for the macaroni.

VELVEETA Italian Sausage Bake

Prep: 25 min. • Total: 45 min.

1½ cups small penne pasta, uncooked

1 lb. Italian sausage, casings removed

4 small zucchini, halved lengthwise, sliced

1 red or green bell pepper, chopped

1 can (8 oz.) pizza sauce

½ lb. (8 oz.) **VELVEETA** Pasteurized Prepared Cheese Product, cut into ½-inch cubes

1½ cups **KRAFT** 100% Grated Parmesan Cheese

PREHEAT oven to 350°F. Cook pasta as directed on package. Meanwhile, brown sausage in large deep skillet on medium-high heat, stirring occasionally to break up the sausage. Drain; return sausage to skillet. Add zucchini, peppers and pizza sauce; stir until well blended. Cook 5 to 6 min. or until vegetables are tender, stirring occasionally. Drain pasta. Add to sausage mixture along with the **VELVEETA**; stir until well blended.

SPOON into 13×9-inch baking dish sprayed with nonstick cooking spray; sprinkle with Parmesan cheese.

BAKE 15 to 20 min. or until heated through.

Makes 6 servings.

KID FRIENDLY:

Prepare as directed, substituting 1 lb. lean ground beef for the sausage and 1 cup *each* shredded carrots and zucchini for the 3 cups sliced zucchini. Also, try using a fun pasta shape, such as wagon wheels.

VARIATION–VELVEETA SAUSAGE AND RICE CASSEROLE:

Omit pasta. Prepare as directed, adding 1½ cups uncooked instant white rice and 1½ cups water to the meat mixture along with the VELVEETA. Increase the baking time to 35 to 40 min. or until rice is tender and casserole is heated through. Makes 8 servings.

VELVEETA Baked Spaghetti Squares

Prep: 15 min. ● Total: 50 min.

4 eggs

¼ cup milk

1 pkg. (16 oz.) spaghetti, cooked, drained

1 green bell pepper, chopped

1 can (7 oz.) mushroom pieces and stems, drained

1 small onion, chopped

½ lb. (8 oz.) **VELVEETA** Pasteurized Prepared Cheese Product, cut into ½-inch cubes

½ cup **KRAFT** 100% Grated Parmesan Cheese

1 jar (26 oz.) spaghetti sauce, warmed

PREHEAT oven to 350°F. Beat eggs and milk in large bowl with wire whisk until well blended. Add spaghetti, peppers, mushrooms, onions, **VELVEETA** and Parmesan cheese.

SPOON into 13×9-inch baking dish sprayed with cooking spray; press into dish with back of spoon.

BAKE 30 to 35 min. or until heated through. Cut into 8 squares. Serve each square topped with about ¼ cup of the spaghetti sauce.

Makes 8 servings.

VARIATION:

Prepare as directed, using VELVEETA Made with 2% Milk Reduced Fat Pasteurized Prepared Cheese Product and substituting 1 cup cholesterol-free egg product for the 4 eggs.

Crowd-Pleasing Entrées

Cheesy Chicken & Broccoli Bake

Prep: 10 min. ● Total: 40 min.

1 pkg. (6 oz.) **STOVE TOP** Stuffing Mix for Chicken

1½ lb. boneless, skinless chicken breasts, cut into 1-inch pieces

1 pkg. (16 oz.) frozen broccoli florets, thawed, drained

1 can (10¾ oz.) reduced-sodium condensed cream of chicken soup

½ lb. (8 oz.) **VELVEETA** Pasteurized Prepared Cheese Product, cut into ½-inch cubes

PREHEAT oven to 400°F. Prepare stuffing mix as directed on package.

MEANWHILE, combine remaining ingredients in 13×9-inch baking dish. Top with stuffing.

BAKE 30 min. or until chicken is cooked through.

Makes 6 servings.

SUBSTITUTE:

Substitute ¾ cup CHEEZ WHIZ Cheese Dip for the cubed VELVEETA.

VARIATION:

Prepare as directed, using VELVEETA Made With 2% Milk Reduced Fat Pasteurized Cheese Product.

Chicken Fiesta Chili Mac

Prep: 15 min. • Total: 35 min.

1½ cups elbow macaroni, uncooked

1 lb. boneless, skinless chicken breasts, cut into strips

1 can (15 oz.) chili with beans

½ cup chopped green bell peppers

2 cloves garlic, minced

½ lb. (8 oz.) **VELVEETA** Pasteurized Prepared Cheese Product, cut into ½-inch cubes

½ cup **TACO BELL® HOME ORIGINALS®** Thick 'N Chunky Salsa

PREHEAT oven to 350°F. Cook macaroni as directed on package. Meanwhile, cook chicken in large nonstick skillet sprayed with cooking spray 5 to 7 min. or until cooked through, stirring frequently.

DRAIN macaroni. Add to chicken in skillet. Stir in chili, peppers, garlic, **VELVEETA** and salsa. Spoon into 13×9-inch baking dish sprayed with nonstick cooking spray.

BAKE 20 min. or until heated through. Stir before serving.

Makes 6 servings.

JAZZ IT UP:

For added heat, add 1 tsp. hot pepper sauce to the chicken mixture before spooning into prepared baking dish.

SERVING SUGGESTION:

Serve this family-pleasing main dish with a crisp tossed green salad.

TACO BELL® and HOME ORIGINALS® are trademarks owned and licensed by Taco Bell Corp.

VELVEETA BBQ Bacon Cheeseburger Mac

Prep: 10 min. ● Total: 25 min.

1½ lb. ground beef

1 small onion, chopped

½ cup **BULL'S-EYE** or **KRAFT** Original Barbecue Sauce

2¾ cups water

2 cups (8 oz.) elbow macaroni, uncooked

½ lb. (8 oz.) **VELVEETA** Pasteurized Prepared Cheese Product, cut into ½-inch cubes

1 large tomato, chopped

½ cup **OSCAR MAYER** Real Bacon Recipe Pieces

BROWN meat with onion in large skillet on medium heat; drain. Add barbecue sauce and water; mix well. Bring to boil. Add macaroni; cook 8 to 10 min. or until macaroni is tender, stirring occasionally.

STIR in **VELVEETA**; cook until **VELVEETA** is completely melted and mixture is well blended, stirring occasionally.

TOP with the tomatoes and bacon pieces.

Makes 6 servings.

SERVING SUGGESTION:
Serve with a crisp green vegetable, such as steamed broccoli.

STORAGE KNOW-HOW:
Store ground meats in coldest part of refrigerator for up to 2 days. Make sure raw juices do not touch other foods. Ground meat can be wrapped airtight and frozen for up to 3 months.

SUBSTITUTE:
Substitute rotini for the elbow macaroni.

VELVEETA Easy Beef Taco Salad

Prep: 10 min. • Total: 30 min.

- 1 lb. ground beef
- 1 small onion, chopped
- 1 pkg. (1¼ oz.) **TACO BELL® HOME ORIGINALS®** Taco Seasoning Mix
- ¾ cup water
- 1 pkg. (10 oz.) frozen corn
- ½ lb. (8 oz.) **VELVEETA** Pasteurized Prepared Cheese Product, cut into ½-inch cubes
- 1 bag (8 oz.) shredded iceberg lettuce (about 4½ cups)
- 1 large tomato, chopped
- 6 oz. tortilla chips (about 9 cups)

BROWN meat with onions in large skillet on medium-high heat; drain. Add seasoning mix and water; cook as directed on package.

STIR in corn and **VELVEETA**; cover. Cook on low heat 5 min. or until **VELVEETA** is completely melted and mixture is well blended, stirring frequently.

SPOON over lettuce just before serving; top with tomatoes. Serve with tortilla chips.

Makes 6 servings, 1 cup each.

SIZE-WISE:

Let your kids help assemble these main-dish salads. As a bonus, they'll also learn about portion sizes.

SUBSTITUTE:

Substitute thawed frozen LOUIS RICH Pure Ground Turkey for the ground beef.

TACO BELL® and HOME ORIGINALS® are trademarks owned and licensed by Taco Bell Corp.

VELVEETA Tex-Mex Beef and Potatoes

Prep: 10 min. • Total: 30 min.

- 1 lb. ground beef
- 1 red or green bell pepper, chopped
- 1 onion, chopped
- 1 pkg. (1¼ oz.) **TACO BELL® HOME ORIGINALS®** Taco Seasoning Mix
- ½ cup water
- 4 cups frozen Southern-style hash browns (cubed not shredded variety)
- 1 pkg. (10 oz.) frozen corn
- ½ lb. (8 oz.) **VELVEETA** Pasteurized Prepared Cheese Product, cut into ½-inch cubes

PREHEAT oven to 350°F. Brown meat with peppers and onions in large skillet on medium-high heat, stirring occasionally to break up the meat; drain. Return meat mixture to skillet.

ADD taco seasoning mix and water; stir until well blended. Stir in potatoes, corn and **VELVEETA**. Spoon into 13×9-inch baking dish; cover with foil.

BAKE 20 min. Uncover; stir gently. Bake, uncovered, an additional 15 min. or until heated through.

Makes 6 servings, about 1⅓ cups each.

SIZE-WISE:

Need to feed a hungry family of 6? This tasty main dish can be on the table in a matter of minutes!

USE YOUR STOVE:

Brown meat with peppers and onions in large skillet as directed; drain and return to skillet. Add taco seasoning mix, water, potatoes and corn; stir until blended. Cover and cook on medium high heat 5 to 7 min. or until potatoes are tender. Stir in VELVEETA; cook, uncovered, until VELVEETA is completely melted and mixture is well blended, stirring occasionally.

TACO BELL® and HOME ORIGINALS® are trademarks owned and licensed by Taco Bell Corp.

Crowd-Pleasing Entrées

Cheesy Cheeseburger Mac

Prep: 10 min. ● Total: 30 min.

1 lb. ground beef
1¼ cups water
¾ cup milk
⅓ cup ketchup
1 pkg. (12 oz.) **VELVEETA** Shells & Cheese Dinner
1 large tomato, chopped

BROWN meat in large skillet; drain.

ADD water, milk and ketchup; mix well. Bring to boil. Stir in Shell Macaroni; return to boil. Reduce heat to medium-low; cover. Simmer 10 min. or until macaroni is tender.

STIR in Cheese Sauce and tomatoes until well blended. Cook until heated through, stirring occasionally.

Makes 4 servings.

SERVING SUGGESTION:

Serve with a crisp mixed green salad tossed with your favorite KRAFT Dressing.

SUBSTITUTE:

Prepare as directed, substituting 2 pouches (1 cup each) frozen BOCA Meatless Ground Burger for the browned ground beef.

VELVEETA Down-Home Macaroni & Cheese

Prep: 20 min. ● Total: 40 min.

¼ cup (½ stick) butter or margarine, divided

¼ cup all-purpose flour

1 cup milk

½ lb. (8 oz.) **VELVEETA** Pasteurized Prepared Cheese Product, cut into ½-inch cubes

2 cups elbow macaroni, cooked, drained

½ cup **KRAFT** Shredded Cheddar Cheese

¼ cup crushed **RITZ** Crackers

PREHEAT oven to 350°F. Melt 3 Tbsp. of the butter in medium saucepan on low heat. Add flour; mix well. Cook 2 min., stirring constantly. Gradually add milk, stirring until well blended. Cook on medium heat until mixture boils and thickens, stirring constantly. Add **VELVEETA**; cook until melted, stirring frequently. Add macaroni; mix lightly.

SPOON into lightly greased 2-qt. casserole dish; sprinkle with shredded cheese. Melt remaining 1 Tbsp. butter; toss with cracker crumbs. Sprinkle over casserole.

BAKE 20 min. or until heated through.

Makes 5 servings, 1 cup each.

HEALTHY LIVING:

Save 60 calories, 9g fat, and 5g saturated fat per serving by preparing with fat-free milk, VELVEETA Made With 2% Milk Reduced Fat Pasteurized Prepared Cheese Product, KRAFT 2% Milk Shredded Reduced Fat Cheddar Cheese and RITZ Reduced Fat Crackers.

JAZZ IT UP:

Stir in ¼ cup OSCAR MAYER Real Bacon Bits with the cooked macaroni.

Hot 'n Hearty Soups and Sandwiches

HOT, CHEESY SOUPS AND SANDWICHES
PERFECT FOR PARTY TIME OR ANY TIME

VELVEETA BBQ Turkey Griller

Prep: 10 min • Total: 16 min.

- 8 slices bread
- ¼ lb. (4 oz.) **VELVEETA** Pasteurized Prepared Cheese Product, cut into 8 slices
- 24 slices **OSCAR MAYER** Shaved Smoked Turkey Breast
- ½ of a small onion, sliced, separated into rings
- ¼ cup **BULL'S-EYE** Original Barbecue Sauce
- 8 tsp. margarine, softened

TOP each of 4 of the bread slices with 2 **VELVEETA** slices, 6 turkey slices, 2 or 3 onion rings and 1 Tbsp. barbecue sauce; cover with second bread slice.

SPREAD outsides of sandwiches evenly with margarine.

COOK in skillet on medium heat 3 min. on each side or until golden brown on both sides.

Makes 4 servings, 1 sandwich each.

SUBSTITUTE:

Prepare as directed, using whole-grain bread and VELVEETA Made With 2% Milk Reduced Fat Pasteurized Prepared Cheese Product.

MAKE IT EASY:

For easier slicing of VELVEETA, give the knife blade or cheese slicer's roller bar a light mist of nonstick cooking spray first. No more sticking!

VELVEETA Ultimate Grilled Cheese

Prep: 5 min. • Total: 11 min.

- 8 slices white bread
- 6 oz. **VELVEETA** Pasteurized Prepared Cheese Product, sliced
- 8 tsp. soft margarine

TOP 4 of the bread slices with **VELVEETA**. Cover with remaining bread slices.

SPREAD outsides of sandwiches evenly with margarine.

COOK in skillet on medium heat 3 min. on each side or until golden brown on both sides.

Makes 4 servings, 1 sandwich each.

SUBSTITUTE:

Prepare as directed, using VELVEETA Made With 2% Milk Reduced Fat Pasteurized Prepared Cheese Product.

Cheesy Spinach Soup

Prep: 15 min. ● Total: 25 min.

1 Tbsp. soft reduced calorie margarine

¼ cup chopped onions

2 cups fat-free milk

½ lb. (8 oz.) **VELVEETA** Made With 2% Milk Reduced Fat Pasteurized Prepared Cheese Product, cut into ½-inch cubes

1 pkg. (10 oz.) frozen chopped spinach, cooked, well drained

⅛ tsp. ground nutmeg

dash pepper

MELT margarine in medium saucepan on medium heat. Add onions; cook and stir until tender.

ADD remaining ingredients; cook on low heat until **VELVEETA** is melted and soup is heated through, stirring occasionally.

Makes 4 servings, about 1 cup each.

SIZE-WISE:

Savor the flavor of this cheesy soup while keeping portion size in mind.

SUBSTITUTE:

Prepare as directed, substituting frozen chopped broccoli for the spinach.

USE YOUR MICROWAVE:

Microwave onions and margarine in medium microwavable bowl on HIGH 30 sec. to 1 min. or until onions are tender. Stir in remaining ingredients. Microwave 6 to 8 min. or until VELVEETA is completely melted and soup is heated through, stirring every 3 min.

VELVEETA Sweet & Cheesy Panini

Prep: 10 min. • Total: 16 min.

- 8 slices bread
- ¼ lb. (4 oz.) **VELVEETA** Pasteurized Prepared Cheese Product, cut into 8 slices
- 24 slices **OSCAR MAYER** Shaved Brown Sugar Ham
- 1 Granny Smith apple, thinly sliced
- 8 tsp. margarine, softened
- 2 tsp. powdered sugar

COVER each of 4 of the bread slices with 2 slices of **VELVEETA**, 6 ham slices and one-fourth of the apples. Top with remaining bread slices.

SPREAD outsides of sandwiches evenly with margarine.

COOK in skillet on medium heat for 3 min. on each side or until **VELVEETA** is melted and sandwiches are golden brown on both sides. Place on serving plates; sprinkle lightly with powdered sugar.

*Makes 4 servings,
1 sandwich each.*

SUBSTITUTE:

Prepare as directed, using whole grain bread and VELVEETA Made With 2% Milk Reduced Fat Pasteurized Prepared Cheese Product.

SERVING SUGGESTION:

Serve with a tossed green salad topped with your favorite KRAFT Dressing, such as Light Reduced Fat Ranch.

VELVEETA Salsa Joe Sandwich

Prep: 10 min. ● Total: 25 min.

1 lb. lean ground beef

¼ cup chopped onions

6 oz. **VELVEETA** Pasteurized Prepared Cheese Product, cut into
½-inch cubes

1 cup **TACO BELL® HOME ORIGINALS®** Thick 'N Chunky Salsa

6 kaiser rolls, partially split

BROWN meat with onions in large skillet on medium heat; drain.
Return to skillet.

ADD VELVEETA and salsa; mix well. Reduce heat to medium-low;
cook until **VELVEETA** is completely melted and mixture is well
blended, stirring frequently.

SPOON evenly into rolls just before serving.

Makes 6 servings, 1 sandwich each.

VELVEETA CHEESY TACOS:

Omit rolls. Prepare meat mixture as directed; spoon into 12 TACO BELL®
HOME ORIGINALS® Taco Shells. Top with shredded lettuce and chopped
tomatoes. Makes 6 servings, 2 tacos each.

JAZZ IT UP:

For extra heat, prepare as directed using VELVEETA Mild Mexican
Pasteurized Prepared Cheese Product with Jalapeño Peppers.

CREATIVE LEFTOVERS:

Cover and refrigerate any leftover meat mixture. Reheat, then spoon over
split hot baked potatoes.

VELVEETA Bacon Burgers

Prep: 10 min. ● Total: 24 min.

- 1 lb. extra-lean ground beef
- 2 Tbsp. **KRAFT** Light House Italian Reduced Fat Dressing
- ¼ lb. (4 oz.) **VELVEETA** Made With 2% Milk Reduced Fat Pasteurized Prepared Cheese Product, cut into 4 slices
- 4 tsp. **OSCAR MAYER** Real Bacon Recipe Pieces
- 4 whole wheat hamburger buns, split

SHAPE ground beef into 4 patties. Cook in dressing in skillet on medium-high heat 10 to 12 min. or until burgers are cooked through (160°F), turning after 5 min.

TOP with **VELVEETA** and bacon; cover skillet with lid. Cook an additional 1 to 2 min. or until **VELVEETA** begins to melt.

SERVE in buns.

Makes 4 servings, 1 cheeseburger each.

JAZZ IT UP:

Cover bottom half of each bun with lettuce leaf before topping with burger.

COOK GROUND MEAT THOROUGHLY:

Cook ground beef thoroughly and evenly. The color of the raw ground meat can vary from bright red to light pink. Do not rely on the color of the meat to check for doneness but use an instant read thermometer instead. Ground beef should be cooked to an internal temperature of 160°F.

SERVING SUGGESTION:

Serve with bagged mixed greens tossed with cut-up fresh vegetables. Top with your favorite KRAFT Dressing, such as Light Reduced Fat Ranch.

Cheesy Chicken Ranch Sandwiches

Prep: 5 min. ● Total: 19 min.

---

6 small boneless, skinless chicken breast halves (1½ lb.)

⅔ cup **KRAFT** Ranch Dressing, divided

6 oz. **VELVEETA** Pasteurized Prepared Cheese Product, sliced

6 French bread rolls, split

6 large lettuce leaves

PREHEAT broiler. Spray rack of broiler pan with cooking spray; top with chicken. Brush with ⅓ cup of the dressing.

BROIL, 3 to 4 inches from heat, 5 to 6 min. on each side or until chicken is cooked through (165°F). Top with **VELVEETA**. Broil an additional 2 min. or until **VELVEETA** is melted.

SPREAD cut sides of rolls evenly with remaining ⅓ cup dressing; fill with lettuce and chicken.

Makes 6 servings, 1 sandwich each.

SERVING SUGGESTION:

Serve with your favorite fresh fruit.

KEEPING IT SAFE:

Use a visual test to ensure boneless chicken breasts are thoroughly cooked. Cut small slit in thickest part of chicken piece. If meat is totally white with no pink color, it is safe to eat.

STORAGE KNOW-HOW:

Seal chicken in freezer-safe resealable plastic bag. Uncooked chicken can be kept frozen for up to 6 months; cooked chicken for up to 3 months.

Southwestern Corn Soup

Prep: 10 min. ● Total: 25 min.

¾ cup chopped green peppers

1 Tbsp. butter or margarine

3 oz. **PHILADELPHIA** Cream Cheese, cubed

½ lb. (8 oz.) **VELVEETA** Mild Mexican Pasteurized Prepared Cheese Product with Jalapeno Peppers, cut into ½-inch cubes

1 can (14.75 oz.) cream-style corn

1½ cups milk

¼ cup crushed tortilla chips

COOK and stir peppers in butter in medium saucepan on medium heat until crisp-tender. Reduce heat to low.

ADD cream cheese; cook until melted, stirring frequently. Stir in **VELVEETA**, corn and milk. Cook until **VELVEETA** is completely melted and soup is heated through, stirring occasionally.

SERVE topped with the crushed chips.

Makes 6 servings, ¾ cup each.

SERVING SUGGESTION:

Serve with a mixed green salad and slice of whole wheat bread.

USE YOUR MICROWAVE:

Microwave peppers and butter in medium microwavable bowl on HIGH 1 min. or until crisp-tender. Add cream cheese and milk; cover with plastic wrap. Turn back one corner to vent. Microwave 2 to 3 min. or until cream cheese is melted, stirring after 2 min. Stir in VELVEETA and corn. Microwave 4 to 5 min. or until VELVEETA is completely melted and mixture is well blended, stirring every 2 min.

JAZZ IT UP:

Garnish with chopped cilantro for a burst of extra-fresh flavor.

SOUPS

SANDWICHES